This Book

RAWR!

Belongs To:

━━ ━━ ━━ ━━ ━━ ━━ ━━ ━━ ━━ ━━ ━━ ━━ ━━ ━━ ━━

**Thank you for your purchase,
if you like the product, please don't forget
to give me a review on my amazon product page**

EORAPTOR

231 MYA, Late Triassic, Argentina

ne of the first dinosaurs, eoraptor was a small, swift omnivore that stood on two legs. Its name means "dawn plunderer." During its time, dinosaurs were not yet the dominant land vertebrates they would eventually become.

MELANOROSAURUS

216-201 MYA, Late Triassic, South Africa

This animal was a basal sauropod, which, at about 8 meters long, was still small compared to the behemoths the future would usher in. Despite this, it had a heavily-built body and robust limbs, and a small head that would be traits shared by many sauropods to come.

COELOPHYSIS

203-196 MYA, Late Triassic to Early Jurassic, United States

This 3 meter long speedy carnivore had eyesight akin to the hawks and eagles of today, with excellent color vision and poor low-light vision. They hunted small, fast moving prey, and may have ventured into shallow water to catch fish. Their environment consisted of floodplains with distinct wet and dry seasons.

SCUTELLOSAURUS

196 MYA, Early Jurassic, United States

This early "little shielded lizard" had several hundred osteoderms running down the length of its back and tail.
Despite this, it was a small, lightly-built bipedal herbivore, at just over a meter long.

BARAPASAURUS

196-183 MYA, Early Jurassic, India

sauropod with one of the most completely known skeleton of its group in the early Jurassic, the size of Barapasaurus was comparable to later
embers, at around 14 meters in length. Even this early in sauropod evolution, the skeleton showed hints of developing ways of overcoming
the stresses of its body's sheer weight, such as the hollowing of the vertebrae.

DILOPHOSAURUS

193 MYA, Early Jurassic, United States

his predator was one of the largest carnivorous dinosaurs of its time, at 7 meters in length. No significant differences have been found tween fossils that would suggest dimorphism between male and female skeletal systems. Because of similarities it seems to share with spinosaurs and its proximity to water in life, it has been suggested that it was a piscivore.

KULINDADROMEUS

169-144 MYA, Middle to Late Jurassic, Russia

This little herbivore was 1.5 meters long, and had a body covered by a layer of dinofuzz, while its tail had a scaley covering. This discovery of an ornithischian dinosaur having a feathery coat points at this trait originating in a shared common ancestor of both bird-hipped and lizard-hipped groups of dinosaur, rather than being exclusive to the theropods.

YI

160 MYA, Middle Jurassic, China

is not only notable for having the shortest genus name of any dinosaur, but for the way its wings are presented. Yi had a feathery coating, d bones at its wrist supported a membrane that may have been used in gliding, with some flapping to control its descent. This was a very small dinosaur, weighing less than 400 grams.

YINLONG

158 MYA, Late Jurassic, China

t just over one meter long, this ancestor to the ceratopsians was a lot smaller than what many of its would end up becoming. The crest wasn't early as pronounced as it would become in time, and this little generalist herbivore was still a bipedal dinosaur. It might have had a set of quills along its tail and back, as some later species would be discovered with evidence of such.

ALLOSAURUS

155-150 MYA, Late Jurassic, United States, Portugal

large bipedal predator averaging 8.5 meters in length, Allosaurus is one of the better-known, and more common, theropods. It wasn't as built for speed as other theropods, but was better suited as an ambush predator in its semiarid, floodplain, environment.

KENTROSAURUS

155-150 MYA, Late Jurassic, Tanzania

This 4.5 meter long stegosaurian dinosaur had a front half that was adorned with two rows of standing plates, and a back half that sported two rows of spikes. Being a smaller member of the group, and having a center of mass that was unusually far back for a quadruped, it was able to rear up on its hind limbs to reach food that was higher up. This trait also allowed it to quickly pivot, swinging the spiked tail at its attacker.

BARYONYX

130-125 MYA, Late Cretaceous, England, Spain, Portugal

aryonyx were specialized in catching and eating fish, and it used both its teeth and the "heavy claw" on its hands to aquire prey. It was obably not only limited to eating fish, or even things that lived in the water, as both pterosaur and Iguandon remains have been found with evidence of predation and/or scavenging.

GASTONIA

126 MYA, Early Cretaceous, North America

...is 5 meter long herbivore was heavily-armored was abundant in the partly wooded areas it inhabited. Unlike some ankylosaurian dinosaurs, Gastonia lacked a tail club, and instead defended itself with rows of bony spikes protruding out from the back. Even for this group of dinosaurs, its limbs were short, and it was wide around the middle.

IGUANODON

126-125 MYA, Early Cretaceous, North Africa, Belgium, England, Germany, United States

anodon were herbivores that were capable of moving about either two-legged or four-legged stances. They averaged 10 meters in length.

h front foot had a spiked thumb they could have used to defend themselves with (or for getting into seeds and nuts), while the little finger was flexible and capable of allowing the animal to grasp and manipulate objects.

YUTYRANNUS

124 MYA, Early Cretaceous, China

large tyrannosauroid is the largest member of the group to have been confirmed to have been covered in feathers. Because of the climate
lived in, this covering was likely used primarily as insulation against the cold environment. They were large, bipedal predators capable of
reaching sizes of up to 9 meters long.

CITIPATI

84-75 MYA, Late Cretaceous, Mongolia

se oviraptorids are commonly used to reconstruct members of the poorly preserved Oviraptor genus, since more and better quality fossils e been documented. The first Citipati were discovered crouching over their own nests, arms spread across on either side over the eggs. This posture is often found in modern birds, and it was decided that Citipati and other oviraptorids were also covered in feathers.

PARASAUROLOPHUS

76-74 MYA, Late Cretaceous, United States and Canada

several other hadrosaurs, this dinosaur could have moved about in either a bipedal or quadrupedal fashion. These animals were rare in the
...il record. Their dental battery was suited for grinding up tough plants, and worn down teeth were simply replaced. The crest has been given
...riety of uses over the years, including display, sound production, a snorkle-like function, and scent detection, though most are outdated.

VELOCIRAPTOR

75-71 MYA, Late Cretaceous, Mongolia

dinosaur was just under two meters long, and, like many other raptors, had a long sickle-shaped claw on each foot, held off the ground.
y had complex feather structures rivaling those found in many modern birds, evidenced by quill knobs discovered on the forelimbs showing
where the feather attachments would have been.

STYRACOSAURUS

75 MYA, Late Cretaceous, United States and Canada

"spiked lizard" lived in herds, and used its beak to eat tough vegetation. Its mouth was filled with a dental battery of teeth that were
tantly replaced as they got worn down slicing vegetable matter. Because of its relative fragility, the extensive horn and frills might have
been used in display rather than defense, though they might have made the animal appear larger to potential predators.

SALTASAURUS

70 MYA, Late Cretaceous, Argentina

genus of dinosaur was the first to be discovered bearing osteoderms, bony plates of armor embedded in the skin. Earlier, sauropods were ght to have been protected from predators simply due to their sheer size, but it seems that further defenses were needed for the survival of the smaller ones. Though they were estimated to have been between 8.5 and 12 meters long, this is still very small for a sauropod.

THERIZINOSAURUS

70 MYA, Late Cretaceous, Mongolia

Therizinosaurs were the first fossil theropods confirmed to be herbivores, not carnivores. At almost a meter long, their claws are the longest of any animal known. The exact purpose of these claws is still unknown, though several ideas have been suggested. These creatures were also the largest of the maniraptorans, reaching lengths of up to 10 meters.

PACHYCEPHALOSAURUS

70-66 MYA, Late Cretaceous, United States amd Canada

of the last non-avian dinosaurs before the Cretaceous mass-extinction, this "thick-headed lizard" was a medium-sized bipedal herbivore. he animal aged, the horns and spikes on the juvenile head would gradually reduce in size, while the dome top and rounded skull knobs grew. dome has been thought to have been used in display, defense, and/or same-species head-butting, but more research is to be done on this.

DEINOCHEIRUS

70 MYA, Late Cretaceous, Mongolia

...rge ornithomimid herbivore, this dinosaur lived in swamps, deltas, and floodplains, and fed on soft plant matter. Studies of its brain cavity ...aled that it had comparable intelligence to a sauropod. Growing up to 11 meters long, its sheer size helped protect it from predation. Despite its large size, several bones were pneumatized to lighten the load.

GASTORNIS

56-45 MYA, Paleogene, China, North America, Western Europe

dinosaur was a large, flightless bird. Originally assumed to have used its impressive beak to disembowel small prey, new speculation points e powerful jaws being used to crack open nuts and seeds, rather than animal bones. Predatory dinosaurs tend to also have curved, pointed claws, which these birds lacked, and the lack of a hooked beak further suggested herbivory.

CASAURIUS

5 MYA-Present, Late Neogene to Quaternary, New Guinea, Australia

e commonly known as the cassowary, this bird is closely related to the extinct elephant birds and moas, as well as the ostriches, emus, and
around today. Their diet consists of fruit, but they will sometimes eat vegetable matter, in addition to small vertebrates and invertebrates.
The cassowary is a generally shy bird, but it may attack with their clawed feet when provoked.

GALLUS

11 MYA-Present, Late Neogene to Quaternary, Global Distribution

ginating in Southeast Asia, the red junglefowl, also known as the chicken, currently can be found all over the world in its domesticated

e. Compared to other birds, these small omnivores' genomes are one of the more unchanged since the K-T extinction event that wiped out

the non-avian dinosaurs.

Made in the USA
Monee, IL
09 May 2024

58172842R00031